Exploring
CALIFORNIA
MISSIONS

MONTEREY BAY AREA MISSIONS

❖

BY
EMILY ABBINK

❖

CONSULTANT:
JAMES J. RAWLS, PH. D.
PROFESSOR EMERITUS
DEPARTMENT OF HISTORY
DIABLO VALLEY COLLEGE

⌐ LERNER PUBLICATIONS COMPANY/MINNEAPOLIS

The images in this book are used with the permission of: © Laura Westlund/Independent Picture Service, pp. 4, 11, 58, 59; © North Wind Picture Archives, pp. 6, 17, 18, 41; © John Elk III, pp. 8, 37, 55; © Eda Rogers, p. 10 (both); Courtesy of The Bancroft Library, University of California, Berkeley, fG420.K84.C6 1822 VAULT pt. 3 pl. XII, p. 13; © Marilyn "Angel" Wynn/Nativestock.com, pp. 14, 15, 16; Photography Collection, Miriam and Ira D. Wallach Division of Art, Prints and Photographs, The New York Public Library, Astor, Lenox and Tilden Foundations, p. 19; © Diana Petersen, pp. 20, 26, 34, 52, 53, 57; The Art Archive/Navy Historical Service Vincennes France/Dagli Orti, p. 22; Zephyrin Engelhardt, *The Missions and Missionaries of California*, 1908-1915, pp. 24, 25, 42, 47; The Art Archive/Musée du Château de Versailles/Dagli Orti, p. 28; © Richard Cummins/SuperStock, p. 30; © CORBIS, p. 32; Courtesy Palace of the Governors (MNM/DCA), 70640, p. 38; Courtesy Palace of the Governors (MNM/DCA), 13742, p. 49; Library of Congress, p. 50 (HABS CAL,44-SACRU,1-4).

Front Cover: © Diana Petersen. Back Cover: © Laura Westlund/Independent Picture Service.

Lerner Publications Company
A division of Lerner Publishing Group, Inc.
241 First Avenue North
Minneapolis, MN 55401 U.S.A.

Website address: www.lernerbooks.com

Library of Congress Cataloging-in-Publication Data

Abbink, Emily.
    Monterey Bay area missions / by Emily Abbink.
       p.   cm. —   (Exploring California missions)
    Includes index.
    ISBN 978–0–8225–0887–8 (lib. bdg. : alk. paper)
      1. Missions, Spanish—California—Monterey Bay Region—History—Juvenile literature. 2. Monterey Bay Region (Calif.)—History, Local—Juvenile literature. 3. Mission San Carlos Borromeo (Carmel, Calif.)—History—Juvenile literature. 4. Santa Cruz Mission—History—Juvenile literature. 5. San Juan Bautista (Mission : San Juan Bautista, Calif.)—History—Juvenile literature. 6. Spanish mission buildings—California—Monterey Bay Region—Juvenile literature. 7. Indians of North America—Missions—California—Monterey Bay Region—History—Juvenile literature. 8. California—History—To 1846—Juvenile literature. I. Title.
F868.M7A24 2008
979.4'7—dc22   2006036849

Manufactured in the United States of America
1 2 3 4 5 6 – DP – 13 12 11 10 09 08

CONTENTS

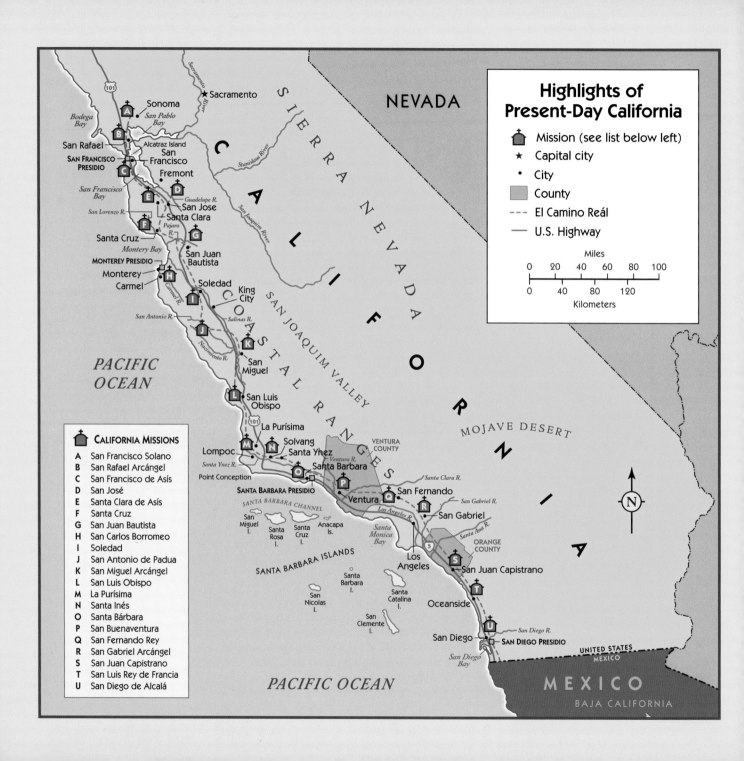

Highlights of Present-Day California

- ⛪ Mission (see list below left)
- ★ Capital city
- • City
- County
- - - - El Camino Reál
- —— U.S. Highway

Miles
0 20 40 60 80 100

0 40 80 120
Kilometers

CALIFORNIA MISSIONS

A San Francisco Solano
B San Rafael Arcángel
C San Francisco de Asís
D San José
E Santa Clara de Asís
F Santa Cruz
G San Juan Bautista
H San Carlos Borromeo
I Soledad
J San Antonio de Padua
K San Miguel Arcángel
L San Luis Obispo
M La Purísima
N Santa Inés
O Santa Bárbara
P San Buenaventura
Q San Fernando Rey
R San Gabriel Arcángel
S San Juan Capistrano
T San Luis Rey de Francia
U San Diego de Alcalá

NEVADA

SIERRA NEVADA

CALIFORNIA

COASTAL RANGES

SAN JOAQUIM VALLEY

MOJAVE DESERT

PACIFIC OCEAN

PACIFIC OCEAN

MEXICO
BAJA CALIFORNIA

UNITED STATES
MEXICO

Sacramento

Sonoma
San Pablo Bay
Bodega Bay
San Rafael
SAN FRANCISCO PRESIDIO
Alcatraz Island
San Francisco
Fremont
San Francisco Bay
San Jose
Santa Clara
Santa Cruz
Monterey Bay
MONTEREY PRESIDIO
Monterey
Carmel
Soledad
King City
San Juan Bautista
San Miguel
San Luis Obispo
La Purísima
Lompoc
Solvang
Santa Ynez
Santa Barbara
Point Conception
SANTA BARBARA PRESIDIO
SANTA BARBARA CHANNEL
San Miguel I.
Santa Rosa I.
Santa Cruz I.
Anacapa Is.
SANTA BARBARA ISLANDS
Santa Barbara I.
San Nicolas I.
Santa Catalina I.
San Clemente I.
VENTURA COUNTY
Ventura
San Fernando
Los Angeles
Santa Monica Bay
ORANGE COUNTY
Los Angeles
San Gabriel
San Juan Capistrano
Oceanside
San Diego
SAN DIEGO PRESIDIO
San Diego Bay

Sacramento River
Stanislaus River
San Joaquim River
Guadalupe R.
San Lorenzo R.
Pajaro R.
Carmel R.
San Antonio R.
Salinas R.
Nacimiento R.
Santa Ynez R.
Ventura R.
Santa Clara R.
San Gabriel R.
Santa Ana R.
San Diego R.

N

INTRODUCTION

Spain and the Roman Catholic Church built twenty California **missions** between 1769 and 1817. A final mission was built in 1823. The missions stand along a narrow strip of California's Pacific coast. Today, the missions sit near Highway 101. They are between the cities of San Diego and Sonoma.

The Spaniards built **presidios** (forts) and missions throughout their empire. This system helped the Spanish claim and protect new lands. In California, the main goal of the mission system was to control Native Americans and their lands. The Spaniards wanted Native Americans to accept their leadership and way of life.

Spanish **missionaries** and soldiers ran the presidio and mission system. Father Junípero Serra was the missions' first leader. He was called father-president. Father Serra and the other priests taught Native Americans the Catholic faith. The priests showed them how to behave like Spaniards. The soldiers made sure Native Americans obeyed the priests.

The area was home to many Native American groups. They had their own beliefs and practices. The Spanish ways were much different from their own. Some Native Americans willingly joined the missions. But others did not. They did not want to give up their own ways of life.

The Spaniards tried different methods to make Native Americans join their missions. Sometimes they gave the Native Americans gifts. Other times, the Spanish used force. To stay alive, the Native Americans had no choice but to join the missions.

The Spanish called Native Americans who joined their missions **neophytes.** The Spaniards taught neophytes the Catholic religion. The neophytes built buildings and farmed the land. They also produced goods, such as cloth and soap. They built a trade route connecting the missions. It was called El Camino Reál (the Royal Road). The goods and trade were expected to earn money and power for Spain.

A Spanish missionary instructs Native Americans.

But the system did not last. More than half of the Native Americans died from diseases the Spaniards brought. Mexico took control of the area in 1821 and closed the missions. Neophytes were free to leave or stay at the missions. In 1848, the United States gained control of California. Some of the remaining neophytes returned to their people. But many others had no people to return to. They moved to **pueblos** (towns) or inland areas. The missions sat empty. They fell apart over time.

This book is about three missions in the Monterey Bay area. San Carlos Borromeo de Carmelo was founded in 1770. It was the second mission to be built. Santa Cruz, the twelfth mission, was established on the other side of the bay in 1791. Finally, in 1797, San Juan Bautista was built.

CALIFORNIA MISSION	FOUNDING DATE
San Diego de Alcalá	July 16, 1769
San Carlos Borromeo de Carmelo	June 3, 1770
San Antonio de Padua	July 14, 1771
San Gabriel Arcángel	September 8, 1771
San Luis Obispo de Tolosa	September 1, 1772
San Francisco de Asís	June 29, 1776
San Juan Capistrano	November 1, 1776
Santa Clara de Asís	January 12, 1777
San Buenaventura	March 31, 1782
Santa Bárbara Virgen y Mártir	December 4, 1786
La Purísima Concepción de Maria Santísima	December 8, 1787
Santa Cruz	August 28, 1791
Nuestra Señora de la Soledad	October 9, 1791
San José	June 11, 1797
San Juan Bautista	June 24, 1797
San Miguel Arcángel	July 25, 1797
San Fernando Rey de España	September 8, 1797
San Luis Rey de Francia	June 13, 1798
Santa Inés Virgen y Mártir	September 17, 1804
San Rafael Arcángel	December 14, 1817
San Francisco Solano	July 4, 1823

An incoming wave sprays saltwater and foam
over the rocky landscape of Monterey Bay.

❖1❖

EARLY LIFE ALONG THE COAST

Early northern California was much as it is in modern times. The land is rich and varied. The Pacific Ocean crashes and sprays against the rugged, rocky coast. The coastal area changes inland to foothills, mountains, and valleys. The Carmel, Salinas, Pajaro, and San Lorenzo rivers flow down from the mountains. The rivers then run through grassy valleys and into Monterey Bay.

Northern California has a mild to cool climate. The coast is warm all year. The Coastal Mountains are warm in the summer and cool in winter. So are the valleys. During winter, snow falls on the mountaintops. Rain falls on the mountains and valleys.

As in modern times, many kinds of wildlife and plants lived in the region. The Pacific Ocean was home to whales, dolphins, and fish. Shellfish, seals, sea lions, and otters lived in Monterey Bay. Trout and salmon swam in rivers and streams. Seabirds, such as cormorants and gulls, made their home along the bay. Geese and ducks lived in the wetlands. Hawks, eagles, and condors soared along the coast. Mountain lions and grizzly bears hunted their prey. They hunted deer and antelope in the mountains and valleys.

Sea lions *(top)* live along Monterey Bay. **Tule** reeds bloom in wetlands.

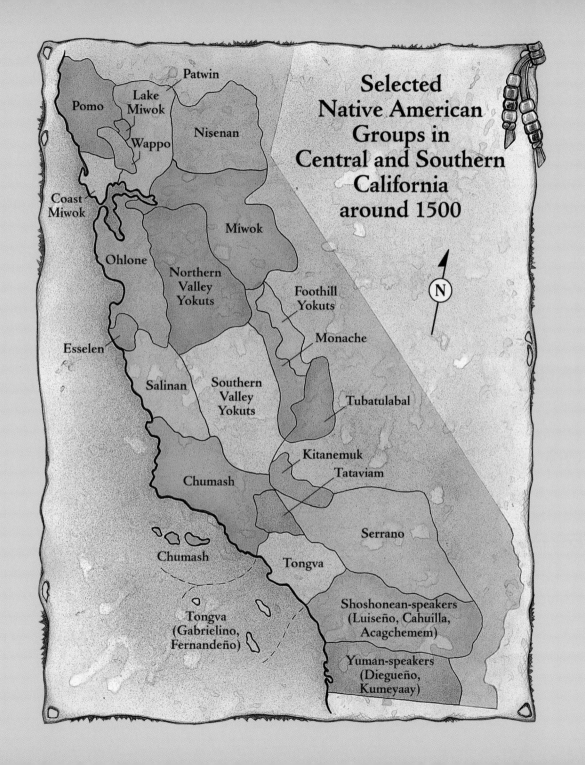

Selected
Native American
Groups in
Central and Southern
California
around 1500

N

Patwin

Lake
Miwok

Pomo

Wappo

Nisenan

Coast
Miwok

Ohlone

Miwok

Northern
Valley
Yokuts

Foothill
Yokuts

Esselen

Monache

Salinan

Southern
Valley
Yokuts

Tubatulabal

Kitanemuk

Chumash

Tataviam

Serrano

Chumash

Tongva

Tongva
(Gabrielino,
Fernandeño)

Shoshonean-speakers
(Luiseño, Cahuilla,
Acagchemem)

Yuman-speakers
(Diegueño,
Kumeyaay)

Oak trees stood in the valleys and foothills. Redwood, cypress, and other pine forests grew up the mountain slopes. Lush wetlands filled with tule reeds and marsh grasses formed during the rainy seasons. These occurred each winter and early spring. Wildflowers grew in bursts of color. Pine trees provided piñon nuts. And the oaks covered the ground with acorns. Nuts, berries, seeds, and wild roots were plentiful too.

NATIVE AMERICAN LIFE

Native Americans were the first people to settle northern California. They arrived in North America several thousand years ago. The Ohlone, Yokuts, Miwok, and Esselan peoples made their home in the Monterey Bay area. The Ohlone lived along the coast, including the bay. This was their homeland.

These Native Americans shared a common way of life. They lived in small villages, or tribelets. Each tribelet had 100 to 500 people. Most Ohlone tribelets had about 250 people.

The Ohlone often wore feathered headdresses for special ceremonies.

The tribelets had eight to twelve different but related languages. Village chiefs and councils of elders provided leadership. Tribelet chiefs and elders included both men and women. With help from the elders, chiefs settled arguments. They also gave advice. And they led ceremonies. They organized groups to hunt, fish, and gather food. Chiefs and elders also represented their people in relations among tribes.

The Ohlone had their own religion. They worshipped nature. It gave them everything needed to live. The Ohlone people trusted their religious leaders. They were called **shamans.** The shamans explained the world to the people. Shamans led religious ceremonies. They gave advice on where to find food. And they healed the sick. They held religious services. The people gave thanks at the services. The people sang, made music, and danced. They also thanked nature daily by respecting it. They took only what they needed from nature.

The Ohlone did not farm. They did not need to. Their environment was rich with food. The Ohlone hunted, fished, and gathered what they needed. Many foods were available during different seasons. Some tribelets moved around in their tribal lands to get food. Other tribelets did not need to move. They lived close to food sources. There, food was available all year.

Nuts, seeds, roots, and berries were the main foods of the Ohlone diet. They ate these foods fresh. And they also dried and stored them. Acorns were the most important of the gathered foods. The Ohlone ground acorns into flour. They used this flour to make bread. They also made a soft cereal, soup, and many other dishes.

The Ohlone fished for salmon and trout. They trapped shellfish. They caught lobster and crab. The Ohlone hunted deer and antelope. They also hunted small game, including rabbits and squirrels. Sometimes they butchered whales that washed up along the shore.

Fish was a staple food for the Ohlone.

Tule reeds and grasses covered the dome-shaped homes of the Ohlone.

The Ohlone usually set up their villages along creeks or rivers. The creeks and rivers gave them a supply of water. They built dome-shaped homes. The Ohlone tied willow poles together. This made a dome frame. They covered the frame with tule and grasses. Sometimes they added a layer of soil. That gave the dome more strength and protection. This kind of construction was simple to make. The willow and tule homes could easily be replaced when it was time to move or when they wore out.

Beads and shells were used as money when the Ohlone traded with other Native American peoples.

The Ohlone usually wore few clothes because the weather was warm. Women dressed in skirts. The skirts were made from reeds, leather, or soft willow bark. Men often wore only belts to hold their knives and other tools. The Ohlone sometimes wore sandals to protect their feet. Many children wore no clothing at all. In cold weather, the people kept warm with animal skin blankets and capes.

Trade was important to the Ohlone. Trade helped them get foods and other things that they could not get in their homeland. They got new tools and knowledge by trading. The Ohlone traded foods and goods with other Ohlone villages. They also traded with other Native American peoples. The Ohlone used olivella shell money to trade. The valued shells were strung onto cords.

The Ohlone were mostly peaceful. But like all people, they sometimes fought. Usually fights were over territory, hunting and gathering grounds, and trade routes. The most fighting happened between Ohlone near the Carmel River and the Esselan and Salinan peoples to the south.

THE SPANIARDS

Juan Rodriguez Cabrillo was a Spanish explorer.

During the 1500s, Spanish explorers came to California. One explorer was Juan Rodriguez Cabrillo. In 1542, Cabrillo claimed California for Spain. He did not recognize that the land belonged to the Native Americans living there. Traveling up the California coast by sea, he saw Monterey Bay. He reported that it would be an excellent harbor for Spanish ships. In 1602, Spaniard Sebastián Vizcaíno mapped the Monterey Bay area. Then Spain seemed to forget about Monterey Bay.

In the mid-1700s, Spanish king Carlos III decided that California should be settled. He ordered explorers, soldiers, and missionaries to the new land. There they were to set up missions. They also built forts and towns. The Spaniards planned to make the Native Americans workers and subjects of the Spanish empire. They also planned to teach them the Catholic faith.

Missions seemed the best way to do this. Father Junípero Serra led the mission plan. He planned to build missions from San Diego to Monterey. These missions would one day become Spanish pueblos if the plan worked.

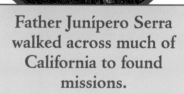

Father Junípero Serra walked across much of California to found missions.

In 1769, he founded the first mission at San Diego. That year, Captain Gaspar de Portolá led a group of Spanish settlers north from the mission. Portolá did not recognize Monterey Bay when he first reached it. But during this trip, he did meet a group of Ohlone people. It was the first meeting between Europeans and the Ohlone.

Spanish sailors recognized Monterey Bay from sea one year later. Captain Portolá set out for the bay area with another group of Spaniards. They reached the southern end of the bay. Again, they met with the Ohlone. But this time, the Spaniards did not move on. Instead, they founded Mission San Carlos Borromeo de Carmelo. The Spaniards were in the area to make it their own.

Captain Gaspar de Portolá arrives by ship at Monterey Bay.

The setting sun bathes Mission San Juan Bautista in pink light. The mission was named for Saint John the Baptist, a cousin of Jesus.

MONTEREY BAY AREA MISSIONS

Three missions were built in the Monterey Bay area. They are Missions San Carlos Borromeo de Carmelo, Santa Cruz, and San Juan Bautista. A presidio at the southwest end of the bay was founded to protect these missions.

All the missions are similar. But each mission has its own history. And the missions are a reminder of California's rich past. San Carlos Borromeo was the headquarters of Father Serra and other father-presidents. The mission and nearby presidio were the headquarters of the mission system.

This engraving shows Mission San Carlos Borromeo de Carmelo and the bay behind it.

Santa Cruz did well at first. But for most of its history, the priests and Native Americans there faced difficult times. San Juan Bautista flourished. It was one of the most successful of the twenty-one missions in California.

❖❖❖

MISSION SAN CARLOS BORROMEO DE CARMELO

San Carlos Borromeo, also called Carmel, was first founded close to the presidio at Monterey Bay. It was the second mission to be built. Only temporary buildings were built. But Father Serra was not happy with this site. He moved the mission farther south to the Carmel River. The river provided fresh water for the missions. And there were many plants and animals to eat. It was also closer to the Ohlone. But the mission was farther from the protection of the presidio.

Father Serra planned the rest of the mission system at Carmel. He wrote instructions. They told priests how they should bring Native Americans to the missions. Father Serra also wrote many letters to priests in Spain. He convinced priests to come to serve in the mission system.

Father Serra tried to make friends with the Ohlone and gain their trust. He offered them goods, such as cloth and beads. Some Ohlone decided to join the mission. They were curious about the mission and Father Serra. Perhaps they liked the sound of religious music. Or they may have liked the church bells. But some Native Americans were forced to join the mission. Others remained suspicious of the Spaniards. They did not trust them. These Ohlone wanted the Spanish to leave their homeland.

MISSION LIFE

Father Serra's plan was carried out at all the missions. Native Americans were brought to the missions, and mission life was similar. American Indians were baptized before they became neophytes. The ceremony included being blessed with holy water. A priest then declared that the neophytes were members of the Catholic Church.

A priest baptizes a Native American baby. This ceremony welcomed the baby into the Catholic Church.

At the missions, neophytes farmed the land.

Some Ohlone came and stayed at Carmel over the next few years. At first, they could come and go as they wished. Some built homes near the mission. The missionaries taught the neophytes the Spanish language. The missionaries also taught them the Catholic religion. The missionaries taught the neophytes how to farm, make goods, and tend farm animals. The neophytes had to obey rules. The neophytes worked at the mission and in the fields. They received food and drink. But they did not receive pay.

Over time, Father Serra and other missionaries demanded that the neophytes stay at the mission. Soldiers from the presidios brought back those who left.

At Carmel, the missionaries and neophytes built many buildings on the new site. They constructed a church, homes, and workshops. They placed most of the buildings around the four sides of an open square. This building plan is called a **quadrangle**. The missionaries

The neophytes made the adobe bricks.

and neophytes used **adobe** bricks to make the buildings. Adobe is made out of clay, sand, and water. It was strong. And it lasted a long time. But it had to be kept dry with good roofs.

Neophytes worked hard. They made many things, including pots, clothing, shoes, and candles. They also tended livestock and fields. The Native Americans washed clothes. They built buildings and furniture. And they decorated the mission with artwork and statues.

At times, the missionaries could not feed everyone. Sometimes crops failed, especially when missions were first started. And the neophytes did not like all mission food. They often hunted and gathered as they had always done. In time, though, the Spaniards improved their farming. Mission lands grew. They spread onto Native American hunting and gathering lands. At Carmel, neophytes and other Ohlone had to come to the mission for food. They had nowhere else to go. There, the Spaniards asked them to join the mission.

VISITORS

The missions were far from Europe. They had few European visitors. Father Serra's mission rules said that only Spanish guests could visit. But at Carmel and the other missions, the priests made exceptions because guests were rare. And sometimes, the king of Spain said they must make exceptions.

Three important men visited Carmel. In 1786, French explorer Jean-François Galaup de la Pérouse stopped at the mission. At that time, the French and Spanish nations had a pact (treaty). The new father-president, Fermín Francisco de Lasuén, welcomed the Frenchman.

La Pérouse and his crew collected plants. They recorded information about the area. They wrote down what the mission looked like. The Frenchmen also described the Ohlone. La Pérouse thought the Ohlone were slaves. He believed the area and its people would do better under French rule.

Jean-François Galaup de la Pérouse was a French explorer. He visited the mission at Carmel in 1786.

In 1791, Spanish explorer Alejandro Malaspina stopped at Carmel. Malaspina was mapping the northern coast of California. He thought that the mission treated the Native Americans well. Malaspina and his men collected plants. They also collected animals, soil, rocks, and goods. Most important, Malaspina helped write down some of the Ohlone languages. For the first time, Ohlone languages were recorded.

Two years later, British explorer George Vancouver sailed into Monterey Bay. He and his men stayed at Carmel. During their stay, the men recorded the construction of a new church at the mission. Vancouver gave a church organ to Father Lasuén. But like the French, he thought the area would be better ruled by people other than the Spaniards.

Mission Santa Cruz

In 1769, Spanish captain Gaspar de Portolá explored the northern end of Monterey Bay. He called the area Santa Cruz, or Holy Cross. He reclaimed it for Spain. In 1791, Father Lasuén selected Santa Cruz as the location for Spain's twelfth mission.

Mission Santa Cruz had the help of nearby missions. The missions gave seeds, grains, livestock, and food. They also sent neophyte workers to Santa Cruz.

Mission Santa Cruz did well at first. It had freshwater, good soil, and many neophyte workers. The gifts from the other missions and the presidio also helped. A large, local Ohlone population lived nearby. Some of these Native Americans came to the mission willingly. They decided to stay. The priests believed they could recruit more Ohlone.

At Santa Cruz, the Ohlone neophytes lived in their own homes near the mission. Mission bells called the neophytes to prayers, meals, and work. The system worked well but only for a short time. Arguments, disease, and natural disaster soon spoiled the Spaniards' plans and hurt the Ohlone.

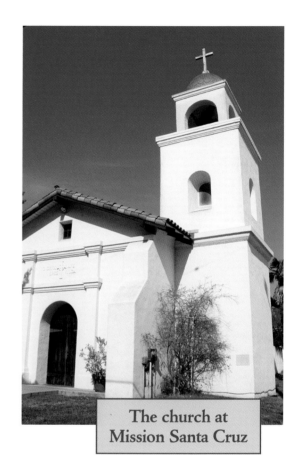

The church at Mission Santa Cruz

DISEASE AND MISTREATMENT

In 1797, the Spanish government in California decided to

found a pueblo near Santa Cruz. Spanish-speaking settlers lived in the town. They called themselves **Californios**. But these settlers and ranchers came with little experience. And they had few materials to make a town or to farm. They expected the priests and neophytes at Santa Cruz to provide the goods and work they needed. The missionaries refused such demands. The Californios were jealous and angry. They stole from the mission whenever they could.

The Native Americans at Santa Cruz suffered from diseases brought by the Europeans. Measles and smallpox were deadly for the Ohlone. They had no natural defenses against these illnesses. The other missions were affected too. Thousands of Native Americans died.

By the early 1800s, the number of Ohlones had seriously dropped. Disease and mistreatment at Santa Cruz took many lives. The Native American population there was the lowest among the missions. At Santa Cruz, priests searched for other Indian peoples to become neophytes. But this only spread disease and violence among the Native American population.

Neophytes are closely guarded by a mounted and armed soldier.

In addition to illness, the Spaniards brought an often violent system of punishment. Neophytes were punished for many things. They were punished for disobeying orders, missing work, and missing prayers. They were also punished if they didn't speak Spanish and if they ran away. Beatings and whippings were common forms of punishment.

The Ohlone and other Indians tried to protest the cruelty. They organized. They fought the Spaniards. But there were too many Spanish soldiers for the Ohlone to win. Some Ohlone protested by speaking only in their own languages. Others worked slowly and destroyed crops. Still others made poor goods. They did this despite beatings and whippings.

A PIRATE ATTACK

In 1818, news of a pirate attack reached the priests at Santa Cruz. The pirate Hippolyte de Bouchard had raided settlements in the Monterey Bay area. It seemed likely that Bouchard and his men would make their way to Santa Cruz.

Father Lasuén told the priests at Santa Cruz to take the neophytes and seek safety at Mission Santa Clara. The missionaries and neophytes safely reached the mission to the north. But Bouchard never attacked Santa Cruz. Instead, Californios raided the mission while the Spaniards and neophytes were away. They took all that they could. Then they destroyed the rest. Although the priests and neophytes tried to rebuild the mission, Santa Cruz was never the same.

Mission San Juan Bautista

Father Lasuén was worried that the area between Santa Cruz and Carmel was unsafe for travel. He decided a mission should be built between the two locations. In 1797, Father Lasuén founded Mission San Juan Bautista. It was built near the Pajaro and Salinas rivers. The mission was the fifteenth in the mission system.

San Juan Bautista was in a rich valley in the Coastal Mountains. The Pajaro and Salinas rivers provided water. There was much wood in the nearby mountains. Many Ohlone also lived in the area.

The site proved to be good. San Juan Bautista became the most productive mission in the area. Neophytes made many goods. They had great harvests. They tended many livestock. The mission always had more than it needed. The priests at San Juan Bautista were able to help other missions. They were also able to trade for goods they wanted.

Neophytes carved furniture at the mission.

BUILDING SAN JUAN BAUTISTA

Fathers José Manuel Martiarena and Pedro Adriano Martínez were the mission's founding leaders. Unlike some, they were kind. They deeply cared for the neophytes they brought into the mission.

The fathers and neophytes quickly built Mission San Juan Bautista. It took them six months to construct the church, housing, and a granary for storing grain. Fields of wheat and vegetables were planted and harvested.

San Juan Bautista seemed blessed. Father Lasuén did not know it, but the location he chose for the mission was on the San Andreas Fault. It was an earthquake zone. An earthquake in 1800 destroyed their first church. But the priests and neophytes adjusted. They built a new church. This church was stronger.

At that time, the new church was also the largest in the mission system. Neophytes painted the walls with beautiful pictures. They made lovely furniture. They created detailed sculptures. And they made a large limestone pool for baptisms.

THE KIND PRIESTS

In 1808, Father Felipe Arroyo de la Cuesta became the head priest at San Juan Bautista. From the start, he seemed different from many other priests. He was kind, respectful, and gentle. The neophytes liked him. Together they improved the church at the mission. They expanded the church. And they further strengthened its walls.

Father Arroyo de la Cuesta and the neophytes also made an Ohlone dictionary. It had nearly three thousand Ohlone words and phrases. The dictionary was the first of its kind. It showed the father's respect for the Ohlone people and their languages.

The father respected other Ohlone traditions. Among them was Ohlone music. He reported the Ohlone people's rich and varied music and instruments to the king of Spain. The father also taught neophytes Spanish music.

In 1818, Father Estéban Tápis joined Father Arroyo de la Cuesta at the mission. He was kind and respectful too. Father Tápis was a good music teacher. He used music to teach neophyte children about the Catholic religion. The children learned better this way. The priest helped neophytes to play

European instruments, such as the violin. Father Tápis also taught neophytes to read and perform European music.

Kindness and respect worked well at San Juan Bautista. Many American Indians chose to come to the mission, even though they had to work hard there. They saw that the priests truly cared for and respected them. The mission had one of the highest populations in the mission system. At its peak, about 1,300 neophytes lived and worked at the mission.

The original designs on the walls were painted by the Ohlone.

An artist's image shows Native Americans, priests, and settlers on the grounds of the mission at Carmel.

·3·

STATE CONTROL OF THE MISSIONS

The early 1800s were a time of great trouble for Spain and its missions. Spain was fighting a war in Europe. It could not send supplies to its missions, presidios, and settlers in California. It could not send money or help either.

At first, the missions did well on their own. They did not need much help from Spain. But the soldiers and settlers soon became angry that priests and missions were doing so well.

The soldiers and settlers soon wanted the mission lands for themselves. And they wanted the neophyte workers for themselves. The Spanish government could not protect the missions.

NEW THREATS AND LAWS

In 1821, Mexico won its freedom from Spain. Mexico claimed the territory of California and the missions there. Mexico created laws that gave greater freedom to many in California. This included Native Americans.

The Mexican citizens believed that they should take control of mission riches. These Californios asked the Mexican government to **secularize** the missions. This policy would force the missionaries to give up control of the missions. It would divide the mission lands. Then citizens could claim them for themselves. The Californios wanted the land for farms and **ranchos**.

The Spanish missionaries fought the secularization plan. But they lost. The Mexican government put the missions in control of citizen leaders. They replaced the missionaries

Families in early California often traveled by oxcart.

with Mexican priests. Some Spanish priests stayed to fight the plan as long as they could. At last, however, they saw the fight was useless. They gave in to Mexican control.

Mexico granted all neophytes their freedom from the Spaniards. The neophytes could leave or stay at the missions. The Mexican government also promised neophytes a share of mission lands and goods.

CIVIL ADMINISTRATORS AND BROKEN PROMISES

The Mexican government began secularizing the Spanish missions in 1833. It named civil administrators. These citizen leaders oversaw secularization in each area of the mission system. They were to make sure mission lands were divided fairly between neophytes and Californios. But most of the administrators were greedy and dishonest.

The Mexican government appointed civil administrators to oversee the distribution of mission property.

The administrators did not divide mission lands and goods fairly. They gave some land to neophytes. But administrators gave most of it to men of power. Or land was given to family and friends. Administrators misused mission property. Some simply stole from the missions.

Trade in the territory was harmed. The ranchos continued to make hides and tallow. Tallow is made from animal fat. It was used to make candles and soap. Hides and tallow were sold to the United States. Rancho owners became rich. But the missions no longer produced the goods they once had. Neophytes became poor. Their people, homes, and old ways were lost to them. Most neophytes were forced to work on ranchos. Or they could take other poor-paying jobs or beg.

THE MONTEREY BAY MISSIONS DIVIDED

In 1834, the Mexican government secularized the Monterey Bay area missions. A few neophytes received some mission land along the Carmel River. Most did not get anything. The rest of the land was given to Californios.

The Ohlone who received land tried farming. But European and American settlers would not buy their crops. Ranchers eventually forced landowning Native Americans off their property.

By 1839, the priests and most of the neophytes had left Mission San Carlos Borromeo. Abandoned, it was looted by Californios. The mission quickly fell into ruin.

At Santa Cruz, Father Antonio Reál gave neophytes as many goods as he could before the administrator arrived. But this was very little. When the administrator did arrive, he refused to give the Ohlone the land they deserved. He let Californios take much of the land instead. They created large ranchos.

Other administrators came to Santa Cruz. They, too, would not grant land to Native Americans. Some were cruel. They beat Ohlone who requested land and other rights. In the early 1840s, José Bolcoff granted what was left of the land to the former neophytes who remained at Santa Cruz. But smallpox killed many of these Ohlone. By the late 1840s, some former neophytes pooled their land and created *rancherías* (small ranches). But in time, powerful ranchers forced these Native Americans from the land.

Some delay occurred in dividing the land at Mission San Juan Bautista. This was because few settlers or ranchers lived in the area. The administrator eventually gave the best lands to non-Native Americans. The remaining goods and land went to about sixty former neophyte families. But the land was too poor for farming.

This engraving was done in 1839. By that time, Mission San Carlos was already declining.

Over time, most of the remaining Ohlone population moved inland. Like other former neophytes, they took jobs on ranchos. Or they were forced to beg. Some formed groups. They raided ranchos for what they needed and for revenge.

U.S. TAKEOVER AND STATEHOOD

In the early 1840s, the United States offered to buy California. But Mexico did not want to sell it. The two countries argued over the area. In 1846, the United States declared war on Mexico. Mexico lost the war in 1848. The U.S. government took control of California. Two years later, the area became a state.

Many people from the eastern United States moved to California. The people wanted land to live on. And they wanted land to farm. In the early 1850s, the U.S. government made Californios and other settlers show proof that they owned their land.

Many Californios saw that they could not prove ownership. They lost their property. Under U.S. law, Native Americans had no property rights. Settlers could simply take their land. The U.S. government honored the U.S. settlers' claims to the lands. In time, the U.S. government moved some Native Americans to lands set aside for them. These lands were called **reservations.** But reservations were often on land that was not good for hunting, gathering, or farming.

During the Mexican War (1846–1848), U.S. naval troops defeated Mexican forces at Monterey. Here, U.S. sailors cheer and salute the raising of the American flag at Monterey Bay.

THE MISSIONS CHANGE AND CRUMBLE

The new U.S. settlers did not care about the missions' grounds and buildings. They looted the missions' goods and took lumber and tiles from the buildings. California's earthquakes also threatened mission buildings.

The U.S government returned the missions to the Catholic Church. Priests and Catholic citizens tried to repair or rebuild the missions. But they often did so in modern styles. Much of the neophytes' original work seemed lost.

In 1840, the church tower at Mission Santa Cruz crumbled. Members of the church rebuilt it. But in 1857, an earthquake ruined the whole building. The people then replaced it with a wooden church. By 1890, the building that had housed the neophytes was the only original structure left.

Mission San Carlos Borromeo was a ruin by the 1850s. It was overgrown with weeds and grasses. Cattle grazed within it. Only birds, mice, squirrels, and other animals made their homes there.

Mission San Juan Bautista held up better than the other two missions. Priests and church members kept up the church and grounds. Father Ciprian Rubio remodeled the mission church in 1865. He rebuilt using styles common to the eastern United States. He put wood over the tile flooring. Rubio plastered the walls, covering neophyte artwork.

By the late 1800s, many more U.S. settlers had come to the area. A town grew around San Juan Bautista. For a short time, the town became a stop for cowboys driving cattle to market and for stagecoaches. But the mission remained in good shape until 1906. That year, an earthquake damaged mission buildings and walls.

In the late 1800s, the church at Carmel had no roof. The mission's stone buildings were crumbling.

This painting of Mission Santa Cruz was done before the collapse of the church in 1857.

•4•

THE MISSIONS IN MODERN TIMES

By the late 1800s, it seemed most people had lost interest in the missions. But a few artists and writers still cared about them. They painted pictures of them. And they took photos of the missions. They wrote stories about them. People in the United States saw the beauty of the missions, even those in ruins. In 1895, a writer named Charles F. Lummis took action. He organized the Landmarks Club. This group raised money to rebuild the missions and other historic buildings.

SAN CARLOS BORROMEO DE CARMELO

In 1879, Father Angelo Casanova decided he could use public interest in the missions to save San Carlos Borromeo de Carmelo. Local people and tourists wanted to see the missions. Father Casanova charged ten cents for mission tours. He raised enough money to replace the church roof.

In the early 1900s, Father R. M. Mestres found artwork that showed how the original mission looked. But he needed money to do the repairs and rebuilding. In 1914, the king of Spain sent Father Mestres enough money for repairs.

In 1931, Harry Downie, a sculptor and cabinetmaker decided to repair the statues at Carmel. The Catholic Church asked him to rebuild the mission church to look as it did in the past. Downie studied the artwork collected by Father Mestres. Downie and other workers then rebuilt the church.

Mission San Carlos Borromeo de Carmelo is the only California mission church that still has its dome.

This is a replica of the original altar at Mission Santa Cruz.

Carmel became popular. In the 1940s, the Catholic Church opened a school at the mission. And in 1960, the Catholic Church officially gave the church the title of basilica. This meant that the church was a place of great importance.

SANTA CRUZ

The neophyte **barracks** (housing) were all that remained of Mission Santa Cruz. The rest of the mission had crumbled. In the late 1880s, people removed the ruins. They built homes over the old quadrangle. They constructed a brick church where the old mission church once stood.

In 1931, the Catholic Church bought all the old mission grounds, except for the neophyte barracks. Two families had received the barracks during secularization. The Catholic Church replaced the brick church with a copy of the original mission church. It opened a small museum there too.

The neophyte barracks were given to the state of California in the 1980s. The barracks were important because they were the only example of how the mission originally looked. Leaders in the California government understood this. The government paid for scientists, called archaeologists, to study the barracks.

The archaeologists removed flooring and paint on the floors and walls. They discovered the original neophyte artwork. They also found fire pits, fish and animal bones, beads, and shell money. These finds helped people understand how the neophytes lived.

The California government then rebuilt the barracks. Visitors can tour its seventeen rooms. Each room is decorated to show styles from different time periods.

Mission San Juan Bautista was restored to its original design.

SAN JUAN BAUTISTA

People did not save the original building styles of San Juan Bautista. Instead, they rebuilt old buildings in styles of their own time period. Or they replaced old buildings with new ones. For example, the church at San Juan Bautista was rebuilt to look like traditional U.S. churches. A tall, pointed steeple was added. And floors and walls were covered over.

In 1906, a great earthquake occurred near San Francisco. The church was heavily damaged. But workers repaired it.

Harry Downie decided to restore the church at San Juan Bautista in 1949. Downie studied how the church originally looked. He strengthened the church walls. He rebuilt its roof.

Archaeologists came to study the church and other buildings at San Juan Bautista in the 1980s and 1990s. They removed layers of paint from the church walls. They discovered the original neophyte artwork. The archaeologists dug down into the ground beneath mission ruins. They found furniture, tools, and even musical instruments. These **artifacts** help people see how others had lived.

San Juan Bautista is open to visitors and churchgoers. A museum features artifacts found by archaeologists

THE NATIVE AMERICANS TODAY

The Spanish missions changed the lives of Native Americans forever. Some of these changes were good. Many were not.

Ancestors of Ohlone peoples still live in the Monterey Bay area. They live like most other people. But they take pride in their traditional ways of life. Many Ohlone have

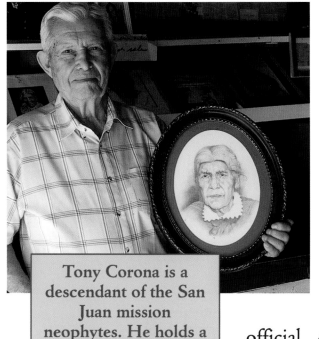

Tony Corona is a descendant of the San Juan mission neophytes. He holds a picture of one of his Ohlone ancestors.

come together to study and save their languages, customs, and history.

The Ohlone have also joined to form their own government councils. These councils include the Amah-Mutsen of Gilroy and San Juan Bautista. There is also the Carmel Band of Rumsien in Monterey, as well as others.

But the U.S. government does not recognize the Ohlone governments as official. And it does not recognize the Ohlone people as a tribe. The Ohlone are fighting for this recognition and a homeland. They want the U.S. government to officially accept them and their rights. They want some of their land back. The Ohlone also want to be paid for other lands and goods taken from them.

The Ohlone are a determined people. They remain proud of their culture. And they will pass it on to future generations.

LAYOUTS

These diagrams of California's Monterey Bay area missions show what the missions look like in modern times. Modern-day missions may not look exactly like the original missions Spanish priests founded. But by studying them, we can get a sense of how neophytes and missionaries lived.

San Carlos Borromeo de Carmelo:

The French explorer Jean-François de Galaup was the first to lead non-Spanish ships to a Spanish mission when he visited San Carlos de Borromeo de Carmelo in 1786. Established in 1770, the mission attracts visitors to the small city of Carmel.

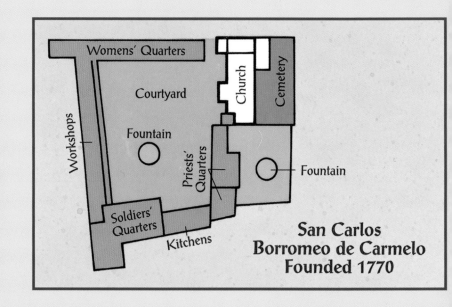

San Carlos
Borromeo de Carmelo
Founded 1770

San Juan Bautista: San Juan Bautista, founded in 1797, was named for Saint John the Baptist.

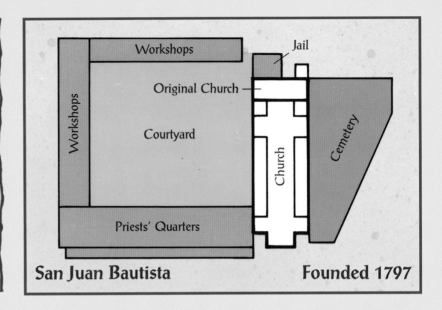

San Juan Bautista   Founded 1797

Workshops

Jail

Original Church

Workshops

Courtyard

Church

Cemetery

Priests' Quarters

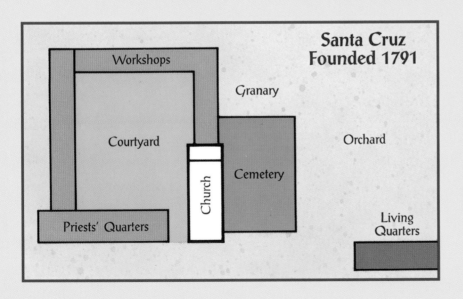

Santa Cruz
Founded 1791

Workshops

Granary

Orchard

Courtyard

Church

Cemetery

Priests' Quarters

Living
Quarters

Santa Cruz: Soon after building Mission Santa Cruz in 1791, the Franciscans moved the settlement uphill to escape flooding from the San Lorenzo River.

TIMELINE

1770   San Carlos Borromeo de Carmelo is founded; presidio of Monterey is built

1784   Father Junípero Serra dies; Father Fermín Francisco de Lasuén becomes the new father-president

1791   Santa Cruz is founded; Malaspina visits Carmel

1793   Vancouver stays at Mission San Carlos

1797   San Juan Bautista is founded

1810   Revolution begins in New Spain (modern-day Mexico)

1821   New Spain gains independence from Spain

1830s   Missions are secularized

1846   Mexican War begins; U.S. Navy occupies Monterey

1848   Mexican War ends; Mexico cedes Alta California to the United States

1850   California becomes the thirty-first state

1850s   U.S. government begins to return the California missions to the Catholic Church; mission buildings are falling apart

1890s-   Missions are restored; restoration continues to modern times

GLOSSARY

adobe: bricks made by mixing clay soil with sand and water

artifacts: objects made by humans, usually from an earlier time period

barracks: simple housing

Californios: settlers from Spain and other areas of New Spain who made their homes in California

missionaries: teachers sent out by religious groups to spread their religion to others

missions: centers where religious teachers work to spread their beliefs to other people

neophytes: a word for Native Americans who joined the Roman Catholic community

presidios: Spanish forts for housing soldiers

pueblos: towns

quadrangle: a four-sided enclosure surrounded by buildings

ranchos: ranches. Settlers in California used land from the missions to create ranchos.

reservations: areas of land set aside by the U.S. government to be used by Native Americans

secularize: to transfer from missionary to state control

shamans: Native American religious leaders

tule: a plant that grows in wet, marshy areas

PRONUNCIATION GUIDE*

Cabrillo, Juan Rodríguez	kah-BREE-yoh, WAHN roh-DREE-gays
Cuesta, Felipe del Arroyo de la	KWAYS-tah, fay-LEE-pay del ah-RO-yoh day lah
Lasuén, Fermín Francisco de	lah-soo-AYN, fair-MEEN frahn-SEES-koh day
Malaspina, Alejandro	mah-lah-SPEE-nah, ah-lay-HAHN-droh
Ohlone	oh-LOH-nee
Portolá, Gaspar de	por-toh-LAH, gahs-PAHR day
San Carlos Borromeo de Carmelo	SAHN KAR-lohs boh-roh-MAY-oh day kar-MAY-loh
San Juan Bautista	SAHN WAHN bahw-TEES-tah
Santa Cruz	SAHN-tah KROOS
Serra, Junípero	SEH-rrah, hoo-NEE-pay-roh
Tápis, Estéban	TAH-pees, ehs-TAY-bahn
Yokuts	YOH-kuhts

*Local pronunciations may differ.

TO LEARN MORE

Behrens, June. *Central Coast Missions in California*. Minneapolis: Lerner Publications, 2008. Learn all about the missions of California's central coast.

Breschini, Gary S. *Overview of Monterey Bay Area Missions*. http://www.mchsmuseum.com/missions.html This site offers information and links to missions in the Monterey Bay area.

Lemke, Nancy. *Southern Coast Missions in California*. Minneapolis: Lerner Publications, 2008. Learn all about the missions of California's southern coast.

Nelson, Libby. *California Mission Projects and Layouts*. Minneapolis: Lerner Publications, 2008. This book provides layouts and guides for building mission models.

Santa Cruz Mission, The. http://www.thecaliforniamissions.com/scruz/scruz.html This site offers virtual mission tours.

Schaefer, Athanasius. *Mission San Carlos de Borromeo de Carmelo*. http://www.athanasius.com/camission/carmel.htm This site provides photographs and a detailed history of the mission.

Schaefer, Athanasius. *Mission San Juan Bautista*. http://www.athanasius.com/camission/bautista.htm View many photographs and learn more about the history of this mission.

Van Steenwyk, Elizabeth. *The California Missions*. New York: Franklin Watts, 1995. Van Steenwyk introduces California missions through clear text and full-color photographs.

INDEX